21ST Century Skills **INNOVATION LIBRARY**

Disruptors in Tech

E-Commerce

Breanne LaCamera

Published in the United States of America by Cherry Lake Publishing
Ann Arbor, Michigan
www.cherrylakepublishing.com

Reading Adviser: Marla Conn, MS, Ed., Literacy specialist, Read-Ability, Inc.

Photo Credits: ©Yuganov Konstantin/Shutterstock.com, cover, 1; ©Diapo scannée/Wikimedia/Creative Commons Attribution 3.0 Unported, 5; ©Carlos andre Santos/Shutterstock.com, 6; ©Syda Productions/Shutterstock.com, 11; ©Andriy Blokhin / Shutterstock.com, 12; ©SpeedKingz/Shutterstock.com, 13; ©Antwon McMullen/Shutterstock.com, 14; ©Terry Granger/Shutterstock.com, 17; ©Ruth Johnston/flickr, 18; ©Dmytro Zinkevych/Shutterstock.com, 20; ©Nopparat Khokthong/Shutterstock.com, 23; ©Ceri Breeze/Shutterstock.com, 25; ©Alastair Wallace/Shutterstock.com, 26

Graphic Element Credits: ©Ohn Mar/Shutterstock.com, back cover, multiple interior pages; ©Dmitrieva Katerina/Shutterstock.com, back cover, multiple interior pages; ©advent/Shutterstock.com, back cover, front cover, multiple interior pages; ©Visual Generation/Shutterstock.com, multiple interior pages; ©anfisa focusova/Shutterstock.com, front cover, multiple interior pages; ©Babich Alexander/Shutterstock.com, back cover, front cover, multiple interior pages

Library of Congress Cataloging-in-Publication Data

Names: LaCamera, Breanne Loren, author.
Title: E-Commerce / by Breanne Loren LaCamera.
Description: Ann Arbor : Cherry Lake Publishing, [2019] | Series: Disruptors in tech | Includes bibliographical references and index.
Identifiers: LCCN 2019006027 | ISBN 9781534147553 (hardcover) | ISBN 9781534150416 (pbk.) | ISBN 9781534148987 (pdf) | ISBN 9781534151840 (hosted ebook)
Subjects: LCSH: Retail trade—Juvenile literature. | Shopping—Juvenile literature.
Classification: LCC HF5429 .L233 2019 | DDC 381/.1—dc23
LC record available at https://lccn.loc.gov/2019006027

Printed in the United States of America
Corporate Graphics

Breanne LaCamera has been working at a global technology company since 2014. She has a master's degree in fine arts from Columbia University, loves writing, and currently calls Chicago, Illinois, home.

Table of Contents

Chapter One
Early Retail Innovators 4

Chapter Two
Online Grocery Shopping 10

Chapter Three
Subscription Services 16

Chapter Four
Return to Brick-and-Mortar 22

Timeline 28
Learn More 30
Glossary 31
Index 32

CHAPTER ONE

Early Retail Innovators

Humans have been participating in the exchange of goods for as long as civilization has existed. The first **retail** shops sold essentials that people needed to survive, while today's stores stock anything from canned beans to luxury watches. From bartering to paying with money, humans have used each other to share and keep civilization going.

These days, retail is a part of our daily lives. We often don't think about it or about the ways in which we shop for the things we need and want. Did you know that when you press an Amazon Dash button, you're participating in retail? Or that when you order batteries with an Amazon Alexa, that's also retail?

Back in the Day

Before the arrival of the internet and online shopping, the only way to purchase items from home was by **catalogs**. Catalog ordering is perhaps the blueprint for modern-day **e-commerce**. Benjamin Franklin was the first to invent the mail-order business in the mid-1700s. Then, Tiffany & Co.'s Blue Book popularized this way of ordering in 1845. This was quickly followed

In 1979, Michael Aldrich laid the foundation of electronic shopping. He connected a TV to a computer using a telephone line.

by R.W. Sears Watch Company (known today as Sears department store), which sold watches and jewelry by mail-in order.

Catalogs evolved to include a variety of necessities and novelties. Have you ever picked up an IKEA magazine? That's a catalog! Have you ever gotten mail from your local grocery store that listed a variety of food? That's also a catalog. These days, retail companies still send out catalogs to customers. Why? According to a study, customers don't directly use catalogs to purchase an item, but catalogs do significantly influence a future purchase. A survey indicated that about 86 percent of women between ages 18 to 30 admitted to buying something after seeing it in a catalog.

The Computer

The evolution of online ordering was made possible by the internet and personal computers, although it wasn't until the early 2000s that both

Many believe that the first online transaction happened in 1994 for a compact disc (CD). The transaction cost $12.48 plus shipping.

were commonly found in people's homes. Tech influencers saw the potential impact that the internet and computers could have on retail. Disruptors in retail used classic retail techniques to develop and invent new **software** and technology that made shopping easier and better.

Auctions

Modern online retail may have found its roots in auctions. Auctions are often used to sell valuable objects like art, antiques, and collectibles, like old coin collections or vintage stamps. Even novelties like Beanie Babies once sold at auctions! Auction items aren't listed for sale at a single price. People bid against each other for an item, so auctions are more successful at selling items for large amounts of money. Can you imagine your teddy bear being sold for a million dollars? It might at an auction if enough people want it!

eBay

eBay was founded in the mid-1990s and started as a way for collectors to sell their valuable items by auction. It evolved from selling expensive items to something more like a **virtual** yard sale. People can buy used strollers at an affordable price or used designer fashion items for less than what they'd pay at a department store.

eBay was an early retail tech disruptor. The company developed an automatic **bidding algorithm** where buyers could set their highest price for an item they wanted and their eBay account would bid for them any time a new bid was entered. In this way, eBay has created a space where **technology** has replaced human bidding and replaced the need for human moderators. Additionally, buyers who load their highest bid into the website can walk away from the auction without having to sit around and wait for the next bid.

The first commercial **e-reader** was the Rocket eBook, produced by NuvoMedia in 1998. It only held 10 e-books in its library. In 2004, the Sony Librie was the first model to actually gain widespread acceptance. People not only read books on the Sony Librie, they also listened to audiobooks and music! The Sony Librie was also the first e-reader to be tied to its own bookstore. Only books purchased from the Sony e-bookstore could be read. All this paved the way for the huge success of today's Amazon Kindle.

Amazon

Much like eBay, Amazon changed the way people bought and sold books starting in the 1990s. People who read a lot could now buy books and resell their old ones without leaving their homes. People were attracted to the convenience and ease of staying at home to buy and sell goods.

Amazon's bookselling success affected large bookstore chains like Barnes and Noble, Books-A-Million, and Borders. However, Amazon went beyond just disrupting **brick-and-mortar** bookstores. When it released Kindle in 2007, the most successful e-reader on the market today, Amazon used technology to change the way people read and bought books. The invention of the e-reader disrupted physical book sales—because now people could carry thousands of books with them on their mobile devices. And they could buy even more books as long as they were connected to the internet.

For the longest time, the word retail only described the act of walking into a store and purchasing something. These days, retail means so many things and has led to countless other inventions and technological advances.

Jeff Bezos

Jeff Bezos started Amazon in his garage in 1994 as an online bookshop. The first book sold on Amazon.com was *Fluid Concepts and Creative Analogies* by Douglas Hofstadter in 1995. When deciding what to sell on his website, Bezos researched the market before settling on books, which he felt would be easily marketable online. He was right! After only 4 years of business, the company added more to its online store, including music, DVDs, and video games.

Amazon is a huge innovator in the retail space, having expanded well beyond books. It has **diversified** and sells everything from music to electronics to furniture and more! Amazon even has its own publishing house, film studio, and clothing line called Amazon Essentials.

Research shows that over 100 million Amazon voice-activated smart speakers have been sold. That's a lot of Amazon devices!

CHAPTER TWO

Online Grocery Shopping

Years ago, just a few grocery stores offered delivery service. But it was only available to those with the means to hire personal shoppers or delivery people. However, with the widespread ownership of personal computers and smartphones, online grocery shopping started gaining popularity.

Grocery Shopping ... Online

Did you know you can shop for groceries without ever leaving the comfort of your bed or sofa? Customers can even choose a time for their groceries to be delivered! Some grocery stores will let you order groceries ahead of time and pick them up yourself, eliminating the steep delivery fees.

Companies like Instacart and Peapod have created online shopping websites that allow customers to order from a variety of grocery stores for delivery to their homes. This has made grocery shopping easier for families with busy schedules. It also allows people to spend more time with their families rather than wandering the store aisles.

In 2018, a little more than 54 percent of U.S. grocery stores have an online shopping program for their customers that can be downloaded to their phones.

"Ubering" Your Groceries

Uber is a ride-hailing company known for disrupting the taxi industry. But, like Amazon, the company is always looking for an opportunity to expand. In 2016, Uber partnered with Walmart to test grocery and package delivery. The service was called UberRUSH. The plan was to pick up and drop off people and goods at the same time. For example, one person might request an Uber, while someone else at home would request groceries to be picked up and delivered. Uber would analyze the best route to take and determine if the passenger or groceries would be picked up or dropped off first. But after several years, the service ended.

Experts project that by 2022 almost 10 percent of all grocery shopping will be done online.

Despite closing the door on UberRUSH, many industry experts believe Uber can jump back into delivering grocery goods due to the success of Uber Eats. Uber Eats, which launched in 2014, is an Uber service that delivers local restaurant food to people. According to reports in 2018, the service has earned about $6 billion in bookings since launching! Sylvain Perrier, an expert in the industry, believes Uber should focus on heavier items, like "pet food and litter," and leave foods like "meats and vegetables" for customers to pick up themselves.

In 2007, about 4 percent of grocery shoppers shopped online at least once. In 2017, this number grew to 23 percent.

According to a survey, about 42 percent of people who shop using a smart speaker, like the Google Home, shopped for groceries.

Amazon, Again

In August 2017, Amazon bought Whole Foods and brought organic food into the e-retail world. Whole Foods' 365 Everyday Value is the store's organic line, which online shoppers can now have delivered through Prime or Prime Now.

Grocery stores have incorporated new technology into their checkout areas. Self-checkout stations, or semi-attended customer-activated terminals (SACAT), have been added to a variety of retail stores. They cut labor costs and increase customer satisfaction by making the checkout experience faster with fewer lines.

Peapod

Though only available in select states, Peapod is the largest online grocery shopping company. Peapod has its own warehouse fulfillment centers and **warerooms** attached to local grocery stores. Founded in 1989 in Evanston, Illinois, Peapod honors manufacturers' coupons as well as many specific grocery store rewards and coupons. In this way, Peapod has innovated the online grocery retail space, making it more accessible to many income levels. The company's app lets customers track orders and spending, making it a budgeting tool as well.

CHAPTER THREE

Subscription Services

In the **subscription** service model, a customer pays a recurring price on a regular basis in order to receive delivery of a product. Publications such as magazines are typical products that people subscribe to. Over the years, subscription services have expanded to include more than just print media—all varieties of products are being offered by subscription. These services have revolutionized the use of automated order-filling technology, which ensures customers receive their orders on a regular basis.

Do you receive a newspaper every day or know anybody who does? A lot of newspaper subscriptions have moved online. Do you know anybody who has a different type of subscription service? You might be surprised to find out your own family has one!

According to a survey, about 15 percent of online shoppers have signed up for at least one subscription box service.

Subscribe to a Meal

Meal subscription services like Blue Apron, HelloFresh, Plated, and Sun Basket send all the ingredients needed for a two-person meal straight to the customer's door. Instructions for how to prepare the meal are included. Customers use the company's **app** to choose the meals they want to receive for a month. This allows customers the experience of cooking at home with the convenience of not having to shop for or plan a meal.

There are even subscription boxes for pets!

Wardrobe Prediction

Another popular subscription service in the retail world involves clothes. Unlike catalog ordering and meal subscription services, where the customer chooses what they want, many clothing subscription services send boxes of clothes that the customer has not chosen. These companies use algorithms to predict what items customers will buy. Many of these algorithms rely on the answers to questions or options chosen by customers on the website. Examples of these services are Stitch Fix and Adore Me. Customers receive a box of mystery options!

Boxes for Everyone

Much like clothing subscription services, many smaller companies appeal to a **niche** community—from dog owners to fantasy readers to crafters and even world travelers! People can choose to regularly receive a set of products for a monthly fee.

Subscriptions can be managed either online or on an app on your smartphone. Retailers have taken advantage of the ease and accessibility of apps to increase sales. A customer can make purchases on the bus to work or from the comfort of the couch. There is no longer a need to step foot into a store.

Are drones the future for meal delivery services? In December 2016, Amazon delivered its first package via drone: an Amazon Fire TV and a bag of popcorn. The technology is still being developed, but the future of online retail delivery may involve the use of drones!

About 60 percent of subscription customers are women.

The Smartphone's Influence

The invention of the smartphone is arguably the most influential in retail disruption. Without smartphones, we wouldn't have apps. Without apps, many of these retail innovations wouldn't have been possible. The very first commercial smartphone was IBM's Simon Personal Communicator in 1994. However, it wasn't until 2007 when the iPhone became more affordable and accessible that real tech advances in the retail space had a platform from which to rise. Every year, smartphone and app technology gets more and more advanced.

CHAPTER FOUR

Return to Brick-and-Mortar

While it seems that consumers rely more on e-commerce and online markets for their goods, Amazon has spearheaded a return to an evolved brick-and-mortar model. This push from Amazon to return to the tried-and-true model may influence other online retailers to open **pop-up stores** and maybe eventually a more permanent store.

Amazon Books

A few years ago, Amazon unveiled Amazon Books. Customers could experience a real bookstore while still paying low Amazon prices. The stores were unique in their design. They didn't organize books like most bookstores, with the spine out and separated by genre, author, and title. Instead, Amazon organized books like its website, with the covers facing forward and organized by popularity. Amazon has several bookstores across the country that have seen wide success.

Amazon's top three competitors are Alibaba, an online company in China, Walmart, and Otto, an online company in Europe.

Amazon Go

Amazon also opened up Amazon Go stores, convenience-type stores that sell fresh, prepared food at a discount. Shoppers use an app on their smartphones to find and purchase the products they want. Amazon has disrupted retail here by eliminating the need for store cashiers and long checkout lines! In fact, Amazon Go shoppers simply purchase what they need using the app at any time, pick up their item during opening hours, and leave. It's as simple as that! The risk to this business model is **alienating** people who don't use smartphones.

Retail is constantly changing. Sometimes it seems like it's evolving past what customers even ask for, anticipating needs we didn't know we had. Advances in smartphone technology have made this possible. What do you think the next changes will be?

The first Amazon Books opened in November 2015 in Seattle, Washington. It stocked about 5,000 books and displayed them with the book covers facing out in order to showcase the titles and authors.

There are over 150 companies that are working to be completely cashier-less by using advanced technology, like machine vision, facial recognition, and shelf sensors.

Some companies have developed smart shopping carts in which customers can shop and pay as they go.

New Tech Alert!

As part of its brick-and-mortar campaign, Amazon developed sophisticated technology for its Amazon Go store. Cameras and motion sensors can tell when a customer has picked up an item off a shelf for purchase. When the customer leaves the store, their Amazon account is charged for the item. This eliminates not only the **middlemen**—like retail and checkout employees—but also the sometimes confusing and frustrating self-checkout stations. To enter the store, customers must **download** the Amazon Go app and link it to their Amazon account. How neat is that?

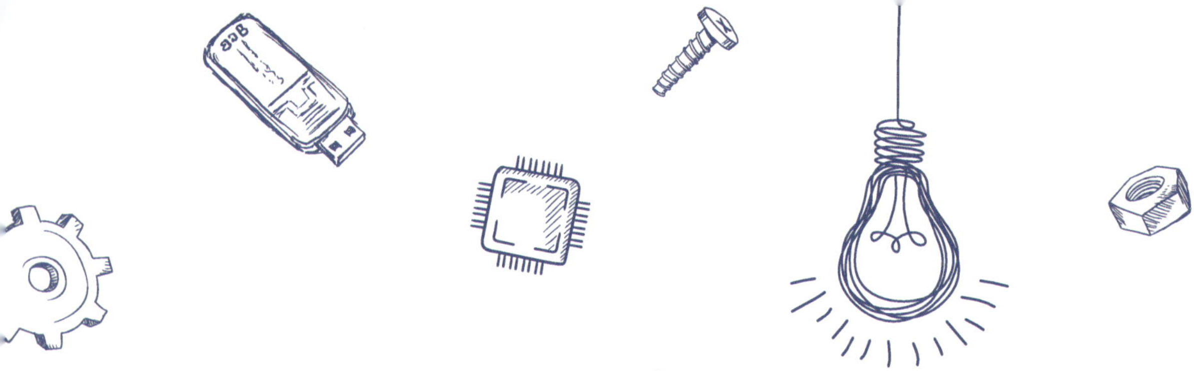

Timeline

- **1744** Benjamin Franklin invents the concept of ordering things by mail.
- **1845** First mail order catalogue is sent out by Tiffany & Co.'s Blue Book.
- **1975** Invention of the first personal computer (PC).
- **1990** Invention of the World Wide Web.
- **1992** First self-checkout station is installed in a Price Chopper Supermarket in New York.
- **1994** Amazon is founded by Jeff Bezos.
- **1995** eBay is founded by Pierre Omidyar.

1998
First commercial e-reader is the Rocket e-book by NuvoMedia.

2007
Apple releases the first iPhone.

2014
Amazon Echo is released.

2016
November: Google releases the Google Home.

December: Amazon delivers its first package using a drone in the United Kingdom.

2018
Amazon opens its first Amazon Go store.

Learn More

Books

Moore, Shannon Baker. *Amazon.* Minneapolis, MN: ABDO, 2019.

Weil, Jamie. *Jeff Bezos: Founder of Amazon.com.* New York, NY: ABDO, 2015.

Websites

Shopify—Entrepreneur Kids

https://www.shopify.com/entrepreneur/kids
Read about kids your age who took an idea and turned it into a success using e-commerce platforms.

Federal Trade Commission—You are Here

https://www.consumer.ftc.gov/sites/default/files/games/off-site/youarehere/index.html
Learn how to be a smart online and offline consumer.

Glossary

algorithm (AL-guh-rih-thuhm) a set of steps that are followed in order to solve a mathematical problem or to complete a computer process

alienating (AY-lee-uh-nay-ting) making something that was once considered friendly to now be unfriendly

app (AP) an application downloaded to a mobile device

bidding (BID-ing) making an offer for something

brick-and-mortar (BRIK AND MOR-tur) relating to or being a traditional business serving customers in a building instead of online

catalogs (KAT-uh-lawgz) books or magazines

diversified (dih-VURS-ih-fyed) to increase the variety of products offered

download (DOUN-lohd) to transfer a capability to an app

e-commerce (e-KAH-murs) buying and selling of goods and services over the internet

e-reader (E-ree-der) an electronic device used for reading e-books and similar materials

middlemen (MID-uhl-men) people who arrange business deals between others

niche (NICH) specialized market

pop-up stores (PAHP-UHP STOR) stores that open temporarily

retail (REE-tayl) the business of selling things directly to customers for their own use

software (SAWFT-wair) programs and related information used by a computer

subscription (suhb-SKRIP-shuhn) an agreement to buy goods or services for a stated period of time

technology (tek-NAH-luh-jee) use of science to solve problems

virtual (VUR-choo-uhl) artificial environment experienced through sights and sounds provided by a computer

warerooms (WAIR-roomz) rooms where goods are offered for sale

Index

Adore Me, 18
Aldrich, Michael, 5
Alexa (Amazon), 9
algorithms, 7, 18
Alibaba, 23
Amazon, 7, 8, 9, 11, 14, 19, 23, 28, 29
Amazon Books, 22, 24
Amazon Go, 24, 25, 27, 29
Amazon Prime Wardrobe, 18
apps, 19, 21
auctions, 6

Bezos, Jeff, 9, 28
Blue Apron, 17
books, 8, 9
brick-and-mortar stores, 8, 22–27

catalogs, 4–5, 28
checkout stations, 14, 28
clothing subscriptions, 18
computers, 5–6, 28
convenience stores, 24

drones, 19, 29

eBay, 7, 28
Echo (Amazon), 9, 29
e-commerce, 4, 5
e-readers, 7, 8, 29

food, 10–15, 17

Google Home, 9, 14, 29
grocery shopping, 10–15

HelloFresh, 17

Instacart, 10
internet, 5–6
iPhone, 21, 29

Kindle, 7, 8

meal subscriptions, 17, 19

newspapers, 16

online shopping, 5–6
    Amazon (*See* Amazon)
    groceries, 10–15
    subscription services, 16–21
Otto, 23

Peapod, 10, 15
pets, 18
Plated, 17
pop-up stores, 22

restaurant food, 12
retail
    early innovators, 4–9
    timeline, 28–29

SACAT (semi-attended customer-activated terminals), 14
Sears, 4
shopping carts, 26
smart speakers, 9, 14
smartphones, 21, 24
Sony Librie, 7
Stitch Fix, 18
subscription services, 16–21
Sun Basket, 17

Tiffany & Co.'s Blue Book, 4, 28
timeline, 28–29

Uber, 11–12
Uber Eats, 12
UberRUSH, 11

Walmart, 11, 23
Whole Foods, 14